A Play of Light and Shadow

The Collected Poems of
Amy DeLaBruere

A Play of Light and Shadow / Amy DeLaBruere

First Printing

10 9 8 7 6 5 4 3 2 1

ISBN 9781936711505

Railroad Street Press
394 Railroad St., Ste 2
St. Johnsbury, VT 05819

To my loving mom,

*for raising me to love and appreciate art, and use it
as a way to express my innermost thoughts.
I have finally found my true art form.*

Contents

"Poetry is when an emotion has found its thought
and the thought has found words."

Robert Frost
Letter to Louis Untermeyer
1 January 1916

I.

Thoughts of Home

Preface

There is one poem in each section that has an especially interesting background which I would like to share with you - either its outlandish inspiration, its basis in history, or its sentimental value.

For this section, Thoughts of Home, I would like to share my threefold inspiration behind "Beside the Stormy Sea". I was walking my dog on a cold, windy day as sheets of rain fell around us. Out on the lake beside my house, the waves were beating against the shore. The fog set in, and a world of grey surrounded us. It was impossible to tell where the sky began and the water ended. It was a surreal feeling, almost as if I had stepped out of my own world and into another. The next day, I read a poem by Elizabeth Barrett Browning entitled "A Sea-Side Walk", which tells of "grey water" and an "unmoving cloud", reiterating this idea that I had been mulling over in my mind. A painting on my wall, "Paul Heads North", by John Smalley, depicts a man walking with his dog along the seashore. The seemingly endless waves and the sheer depth of the sky immediately consume the viewer. The man and his loyal companion seem to be on a pointed journey as the man trudges on with the help of his walking stick, perhaps to avoid an oncoming onslaught of rain from the complexly painted, yet slightly ominous clouds. The artist, my friend and mentor, left the story to be finished by the audience, and you will find my interpretation below in "Beside the Stormy Sea".

Beside the Stormy Sea

A golden head bobs through the storm
And I walk with feet neither dry nor warm
Joyful bounds of paws leave tracks of four
Amidst the frigid rain and uproar
"Will we reach home?" He seems to ask —
We will see through this toilsome task
The many shades of the steel-grey sea
Reach a mass of clouds looming over me
Rain turns to sleet, and sleet to hail
As we charge down this lonely trail
Look there, a light! A welcome sight!
Its fiery blaze transcends the night
Unsure of foot, we make our way
Fierce wind sets weary trees asway
And from it erupts a wild roar
The almighty hands sweep the shore
Content inside, now warm and dry
I whisper a forlorn goodbye
White capped waves beat the sand
Their feral fury drives them, and
We wait and watch it be —
The storm out on the sea.

I Have Seen the Bright Lights of the City

I have seen the bright lights of the city,
And I have walked its lonely, crowded streets.
I have found their gleaming steel castles pretty,
And I have watched as the flawed circle repeats.
Now I leave behind the black and white city
For the endless stars of the midnight sky.
Like flickering candles they hold up the night,
The sweet silence brings to my lips a soft sigh.
In the freedom of nature my soul takes flight,
Away from the truth that man's work will die.
For those unaware I have naught but pity,
I have seen the bright lights of the city.

Ode to the Sun

O Sun, O you brilliant globe of fire,
With your bright light you give the shadows chase,
Force creatures of the night to fear your ire.
The golden flames do lick my frame, my face,
You scorch the bare backs of laboring farm hands.
As you race time from east to west up high,
The sunflowers salute your grand grasslands.
No painter can repeat your setting sky:
Blood reds, blush pinks, rose golds, the skyline turns.
Your nightly twin seeks to trap you in chains,
Each night brings fear that you will not return,
Nor will your mighty rays forever reign.
O, regal sovereign, with your crown of gold,
My destiny, in your strong hands, you hold.

I Lay Beside Still Waters

I lay beside still waters
A lone ship astride the blue
Sailing along the horizon
Content with my one man crew
Deep waters swallow the blinding sun
Shades of blue fade into the sky
The white smudge of a sailboat
Rocks with the waves as gulls pass by
Church bells ring in the distance
A crisp chill arrives as the sky turns gold
All others retreat to the shore
But I lay still, unafraid of the cold.

II.

A Single Spark

Preface

Of all my poems, "Ode to the Violin" took the most time to finish. Most of the time throughout the three month process was spent on translation. Written in both English and Spanish, this is one of the poems in which I take the most pride. I spent weeks studying Pablo Neruda, the infamous Chilean poet, and was especially drawn to his poem, "Oda al Piano". I decided to write my own poem after his, and this is how "Ode to the Violin", or "Oda al Violín", came into being. I began in English and wrote the poem as though it was like any other. As I started the translation process, I found that I had to change what I was saying in order to exude the same meaning and emotion as in the English version. Direct translation gives only a crude and incomplete meaning; I had to find a way to express my poem through the beauty and fluidity of the Spanish language. My Spanish teacher, Margaret Ronald, was a great help to me and was always willing to offer advice or direction. I hope that even if you do not understand Spanish, you will take the time to look over the Spanish version and admire the beauty and exoticness of the language; you will understand more than you may think.

Crescendo

With the first light of day came the soft notes,
On the back of a new spring breeze
They were carried along,
Hushed and unbearably sweet,
The tune begged for the ears of all in its wake.
Merry and cheerful the music grew,
Beckoning spritely gales
To join in with childlike dance,
Oblivious to the light,
Slowly but surely beginning to fade.
Stronger and louder the notes came,
Demanding response from the great beyond,
Cheerful innocence slowly lost,
Singing their undulating story with vigor.
Then a great clash and crescendo of sounds
Marks the climax, the peak,
Amplifying the complexity and skill
Aged as the song prolonged.
Like the calm after the storm,
The intricate melody died to a low hum,
A sense of fulfillment arose,
A recognition that there is more.

(cont.)

There was contentment in the air,
In knowing there will always be a next song,
A new beginning.
A throng of people converged
To hear the end of the sweet, soft melody
Fading into the dark abyss.

The Dance

Notes trickle down like rain on a bell
The strings join in and the drums pound
Sounds guide the body as the music swells
An arm sweeps through the air as if under a spell
And a leg swings in a graceful arc around
A fiery passion erupts from a small spark
Though the music will end in moments hence
The present reigns, leaving a lasting mark
The sky has fallen near to dark
But the dance goes on even in the silence.

Ode to the Violin
After Pablo Neruda's "Oda al Piano"

The instrument laid still,
prostrate on the floor,
the years had done their damage,
the abandonment had caused its decay.
When man and instrument connected,
a spark arose,
with it came music,
lovely music,
two separate entities
joined into one.

The strings moaned,
like stroking the back
of a purring cat,
the bow glided
across the spine of the woman,
giving each curve and edge care:
like a summer rain
as it pours down on the dry earth,
the crashing waves
of the sea at dusk,
like an artist
paints a sunset,
so complex
in its beautiful simplicity,

(cont.)

Oda al Violín

El instrumento quedó quieto,
como un cadáver en el suelo,
los años lo habían deteriorado,
el abandono había causado su degradación.
Cuando hombre y instrumento se conectaron,
una chispa surgió,
con ella vino la música,
música preciosa,
dos entidades separadas
Se unieron.

Gimieron las cuerdas,
como una caricia en la espalda
de un gato ronroneando,
el arco deslizó
por toda la espina de la mujer,
dando placer a cada curva y borde:
como una lluvia veraniega
cayendo a la tierra árida,
como las olas poderosas
del mar por el crepúsculo,
como una artista
pinta un atardecer,
cual es tan complejo
en su hermosa sencillez,

like the comfort
of a warm embrace,
the crisp autumn air,
like a raging river,
beating against the rocks,
stirring up the sand below,
total dominion,
yet still in control.

What had been left for death
gave birth to the purest form of beauty.
There existed nothing more
than music in the air:
no breath was heard,
no sigh of contentment,
no step of a foot,
no yawn from the forgotten
back of the room.
The fingers drew
the sweet, soft melody
from the strings,
and the violin sang
a lost tune
from the world of Sirens.

Until the song slipped off
into the splendid sound
of silence.

como el consuelo
de un abrazo cálido,
como el aire fresco del otoño,
como un río
golpeando contra las rocas,
despertando la arena en las profundidades,
dominación completo,
aún sigue siendo en control.

Lo que había dejado para morir
dio luz a la forma más pura de belleza.
No existía nada más
que música en el aire:
no se oía ningún aliento,
ningún suspiro de alegría,
ningún ruido de pasos,
ningún bostezo del fondo
de la sala olvidada.
Los dedos extrajeron
la dulzón, suave melodía
de las cuerdas,
y el violín cantaba
una canción perdida
del mundo de las Sirenas.

Hasta la canción desapareció
en el espléndido sonido
de silencio.

The Arsonist

Unearthly cracks fill the silence,
Gaunt faces form in the flames,
Empty eyes gleam like meteors,
The dim world comes alight in a fiery blaze.
Smoke billows through the air,
Intoxicating in its swells,
Purging the earth of evil,
But evil it does make.
The devil lives within me,
Fingers clawing toward the flames,
Such an irresistible desire
To leave ashes in my wake.
I speak to voices in the embers,
The flames release their souls,
My only companions in this life,
Abiding in the fires far below.
Through sheets of rain the beast rages on,
Tears through the trees like a chthonic demon,
The blaze is lovely, fierce and bright,
The blaze so lovely, fierce tonight.

22

III.

The Upper Hand

Preface

While I was in France interning for a residential art program, I was introduced to the Dance of Death. This concept dates back to the Middle Ages. It began in Paris, but soon travelled across the English Channel to occupy the British people. Death's commitment to justice and denouncement of greed are the basis of this medieval craze. In a time when the common people led brutal and short lives, the Dance of Death gave them something to hold onto - a promise of equality in death. The notion spread through Europe like wildfire, inspiring many artists to create their own interpretations. Hans Holbein the Younger was one of the great leaders of this movement. He put together a book, titled "Dance of Death", of miniature woodcuts with extremely intricate detail. They depict Death's role in daily life situations as he carries out the fated ends of humans from every walk of life. The woodcuts are rich in symbols of death and Death's coming. This topic piqued my interest from the very beginning, inspiring my poem, "Dance of Death", and I hope it intrigues you as well.

Mad World

Reality fell like the coming of night,
Slowly, then all at once despite
The confusion between friend and enemy,
The sleeping surround breathlessly.
All under the upper hands,
By no choice of his own he stands,
Bedecked in uniform and conformity,
The dark cloud hanging over too late to see.
Broken voices scream in his ears,
Soon one roar is all he hears,
Fear sinks its claws in one by one,
As they shoot down the ones who run.
The poor soldier cries to the skies,
The end is near no man denies,
The world is cold, its people colder;
The night is dark, the foe is bolder.
Echoing cracks split the air,
All freeze and simply stare;
As the metallic rain begins to fall,
The ground bleeds red and tired men call.
A world of robots, a planet of corpses,
In the grass he lays with his forces,
So many lives given in vain,
And he waits for the rain to come again.

Only a Fool Does Not Think to Question

As one foe is vanquished, another will rise,

Darkness has long since fallen,

It toys with the mind, poking and prodding with lies,

The oily surface begins to thicken,

Light becomes naught but a recollection,

It has taken all, its reach vast,

Like a lover's embrace comes the deception,

Fight, fight to the last.

The unknown, a shadowy onslaught in disguise,

Divergence faces eternal extinction,

Conformity is on the rise,

Only a fool does not think to question,

It is at no fault but their own when

Like lambs for the slaughter they are massed,

They fall to their knees in submission,

For them we must fight, fight to the last.

(cont.)

Ares will make hard our brows and focus our eyes,
The courageous still stand while the brave have fallen,
We will inspire fear with our battle cries,
With every drop of blood our bodies strengthen,
Every loss of innocence, our wills harden,
Fight for the future; fight for the past,
Former foes united by the invasion,
Fight, fight to the last.

Thanatos, we can offer you no submission,
To our resistance we must hold fast,
A dark horse shrouded in their haze of distortion,
We will fight, fight to the last.

A Man With No Face

Naught but a player upon a grand stage,
Words spoken through breached lips are not his own,
While sitting before the mirror offstage,
He creates his new face, skin and bone.

Patrons watch, blinded by their lives of grandeur,
Eyes focused only on the show,
Ears deaf to the silent cries of the poor
Man on the stage playing pretend with his shadow.

When the curtain falls, he drops the guise,
The lonely shadow slips through the door,
A man with no face under the starlit sky,
Dark clouds arise and he is heard no more.

Dance of Death

A tempting tune fills the quiet scene,
The pipe and flute summon all to convene,
The dead skip with legs poised in glee,
As they dance in circles happily.
Death is just and Death is fair,
He comes with the whispers in the air,
Unaltered by man's tales of woe,
Fate is all that He does know.
A thief in the night for the usurer's purse,
Greed and power are the man's curse,
The dead drag the fool by his golden chains,
And prance away as the hourglass drains.
The proud knight draws his broken sword,
Death's grip is steel, his icy heart, discord,
The knight's looming defeat deeply galls,
And pride leaves his eyes as first blood falls.
The privileged king mocks the pain of the poor,
Blind on his throne as Death sneaks through the door,
Death steals the crown from his fine brow,
And as His act then ends, He takes a bow.

(cont.)

Death tends a withered old man to last sleep
As the sands of time continue to seep;
He serenades the silence with seductive song,
And lost breath now fuels the whispering wind along.
The seamen hush in silent fright,
And Death grins as men sink into the night,
The sound of the flute joins their lament
While the treacherous sea masks the ship's descent.
Like the piper of Hamelin, He charms mankind,
Young and old, rich and poor, fall in step behind,
Death guides His flock home by the hand
As the rueful dance meets a merry end.

IV.

The Lateness of the Hour

Preface

"As Darkness Descends" was my very first poem. I wrote it on a whim as extra credit for an English assignment, and soon found myself lost in the world of words. We had been studying poetry for a few weeks and had just begun looking at a special form of poetry, the villanelle. This form consists of nineteen lines, made up of five tercets and a quatrain, with only two rhymes used throughout. The first and third lines of the first tercet alternately repeat as the final line of the following tercets, and both lines are used at the end of the closing quatrain. This is an extremely difficult poetic form to follow because of its very structured format and its use of only two rhymes despite its length. I decided to take on the challenge of the villanelle and found my love for poetry in the process. I enjoyed exploring my mind and surroundings for inspiration, searching for the perfect rhyme to depict my thought, all the while finding a beauty and flow between the words. I have come a long way since writing this poem, in both my poetic voice, and my understanding of the poetic world and its history, but this was the beginning, and so it holds a place of honor within my heart.

The Lateness of the Hour

At journey's end the travelers join the crowd,
They wait and watch the clock's long hands go round;
The feet of the old, wizened speaker slap
Against the wetted cobblestones as he
Prepares a final sermon for the flock.

His lips build a stronghold in thought and mind,
But power-driven chaos them surrounds,
A sight of flying swords and battled crowns,
The wars of sword and soul make a ravine;
Red hate burns like the arid summer heat,
And eats away at hope for land and sea.

The quiet man sits on his own in fear,
He quivers with each tick and every tock;
The weary crows look down upon the crowd,
And with their calls of mockery they scorn
The ignorance of this almighty race.

Fair lady lies amidst the sore neglect,
Her former beauty hands of man corrupt;
A fouled lake below a smoggy sky,
The barren trees as they are felled do cry
As poison leaches through her earthen veins.

(cont.)

The crowd of voices shouts into the void,
A rueful tribute to the dying earth;
The mass follows the winding down wrought hands,
A taste of urgency does fill the air.

A single voice can be a flint and stone,
And spread its tendril flames like wildfire,
The passion, it can galvanize a man
For worthy cause, yet when extinguished, dies,
Just like a thousand songs, though sweet for some,
The rigid ears of deaf men do not reach.

But no fine spoken words can save her now,
The bell tolls mark the lateness of the hour.

As Darkness Descends

She calmly awaits the night's embrace,
The cold breath of grief is like a whisper on her skin,
There is nothing left in her but an empty space.

A priceless treasure she can never replace,
The painful flood of memories threatens to begin,
She calmly awaits the night's embrace.

The tears come streaming down her face,
Her eyes close; her mind starts to spin,
There is nothing left in her but an empty space.

She has long stopped fighting the fated chase,
What light could be found in her grows thin,
She calmly awaits the night's embrace.

Darkness has won the relentless race,
On her mind is Death's keen grin,
There is nothing left in her but an empty space.

While a new star enters the vast black place,
The impending darkness rapidly closes in,
She calmly awaits the night's embrace,
As there is nothing left in her but an empty space.

The Rhythm of the Tide

I am lost in an ocean of people
The mighty waves crash over me
Loath to part for a soul so feeble
My battle worn body
Sinks below the deep sea
Frantic hands lift to the skies
The faint sun appears saddened up there
But all aid to me he denies
A sudden taste of despair
Now floods the blustery air
And I begin to drift aside
To the rhythm of the tide.

And So I Say Good Night

'Tis in the deepest calm of the long night
My senses stir as if my life's begun.
A simple candle casts an orb of light,
The velvet glow adorns with golden sun
These quiet trees surrounding where I lie.
To you, deep night, I find there's no compare;
You are my dusk, my dawn, my noonday sky.
Faint whispers of a nocturne fill the air,
Its chilling breath does dance upon my skin;
Soft hum of darkness keep the morn at bay,
For when the streaks of blood and gold begin,
'Tis then you flee and I am left astray.
My eyes gaze wistfully at your starlight,
But dawn is near and so I say good night.

Acknowledgements

My mom and grandma, thank you for your unwavering encouragement and support. Know how grateful I am for your constant willingness to read over a finished poem, or have a deep, philosophical talk over my newest art, history, or culture related obsession. You knew how much it meant to me, and you could see the crazed excitement I had for my work. You both raised me to be creative and questioning, and to see the world with a unique perspective and an open mind. Without you, none of these thoughts could have been put into words to create this piece of art in front of you, so thank you.

Beverly Thurber, you are the reason I developed my passion for poetry. Your faith in me, and your encouragement, spurred me to delve into the poetic world and discover a piece of myself that had been missing before I found my true art form. Thank you for challenging me and always being there for advice and feedback. I am so thankful that I could share my poems with you, knowing that you would always be just as enthusiastic as I was about the underlying connections, the little details, and the deeper meaning of each and every piece. Thank you for nurturing this flame in me. I will be forever grateful.

Kate Linton, thank you for being willing to become my mentor for this project despite the early mornings, many meetings, and long talks over coffee and hot chocolate. Through your guidance, I gained a new perspective on my own work, and also on the world of poetry as a whole. Rather than a hobby, poetry became a lifestyle. Thank you for all of the time and effort you sacrificed to make my dream of publication become a reality.

John Smalley, in you I found a kindred spirit - another person who sees the deep, complex, and beautiful world in which we live. I miss our morning poetry readings up in the gallery amidst the sunshine and the quiet presence of nature. You taught me to appreciate the present moment. This is something that stayed with me and continues to shape my view of life and my ability to discern what is truly important. It was during my time in France that I began to create my own unique identity encompassing all of my characteristics, experiences, and passions. You played such a significant role in this, and I cannot thank you enough for the impact you have had on me.

About the Author

Amy DeLaBruere lives in Newport, Vermont, on picturesque Lake Memphremagog with her mother, grandmother, twin older brothers, and two rescued golden retrievers. Amy considers herself both an artist and an athlete. She can typically be seen running along the long, winding dirt roads surrounding her Green Mountain home. Much of her inspiration has come from her travels. During her freshman year in 2014, she journeyed to Costa Rica where she participated in a Spanish immersion program while doing environmental service work to save watersheds and build greenhouses for struggling families. She also travelled to France for the summer of 2015 to participate in an intensive, residential art program in the gorgeous, rural landscape of the Ardèche region, to which she returned the following summer as an intern. Next, her travels will take her to London, England, in the spring of her senior year. Currently a senior in high school at Craftsbury Academy, she plans to study English, Creative Writing, and Spanish at college in the fall of 2017. A childhood spent reading hundreds of books and becoming an admirer and practitioner of all forms of art has led Amy to her love of poetry. After several years of writing poems, A Play of Light and Shadow *is Amy's first published work.*

www.ingramcontent.com/pod-product-compliance
Lightning Source LLC
Chambersburg PA
CBHW071435040426
42445CB00012BA/1365

9 781936 711505